Your Amazing Itty Bitty™ Dog Training Book

15 Key Steps to Train Your Dog on a Busy Schedule

Melissa Brady

Published by Itty Bitty™ Publishing
A subsidiary of S & P Productions, Inc.

Copyright © 2025

Printed in the United States of America

Itty Bitty Publishing
311 Main Street, Suite D
El Segundo, CA 90245
(310) 640-8885

ISBN: 978-1-959964-85-8

This book is for educational purposes only and does not replace training your pet with a professional dog trainer.

So, You're a Dog Owner, Now What?

Here are 15 essential steps for training a dog while managing a busy schedule

Congratulations on your new best friend! But now that you've welcomed a dog into your life, what comes next? The key to a happy and harmonious life with your dog comes with training. Whether you're dealing with a puppy or an unruly adult dog, training is imperative. Dogs crave structure and love to please you. Training isn't just about teaching basic commands like "sit" or "stay"; it's about creating routines, setting clear boundaries, and establishing leadership, so both you and your dog can live a happy life together.

In her book, Your Amazing Itty Bitty™ Dog Training Book, Melissa Brady will give you the tools to invest in your dog's future and give you peace of mind for a happy, healthy relationship.

You'll learn how to:

• Set clear rules and boundaries
• Master crate training
• Socialize your dog with ease
• Teach basic commands
• And so much more!

If you're ready to build a positive relationship with your canine companion, pick up your copy of this must-read Itty Bitty™ Book today

I dedicate this book to all my family, friends, and clients who have supported me over the years. And to my mentors, Shannon Maeurer, Michael Burger, and Asa Anderson, who believed in me and pushed me to continue to learn and share my knowledge and experience with families needing help with their dogs. Thank you all for many amazing years of training and learning together.

Training is for life!

Stop by our Itty Bitty™ website to find interesting blog entries regarding Dog Training at:

www.IttyBittyPublishing.com

Or visit Melissa Brady at:

www.k9fitforlife.com

Table of Contents

Introduction

Introduction

You have made the decision to get a dog. You're bringing your dog home soon, or perhaps you already have an unruly dog. In either case, training is an absolute must. Learning leadership skills, as well as building the confidence needed to train your dog, will make a big difference in your dog's behavior.

You want a well-trained dog—everyone does. Training is more than just teaching a dog to sit. Most people these days have busy schedules and don't have a lot of time to train their dog multiple times a day.

In this book, you'll find key points about training your dog, designed to work with your busy schedule. Training can be overwhelming, but it can also be easy and fun if you follow these steps and you're consistent with daily training. When you're training, you create good routines, set boundaries and rules, and establish leadership that every dog needs so you and your dog can have a happy life together. After all, training is for life!

Step 1
What to Know About Training

A major part of training your dog is for you to be consistent with training. All commands, rules, and boundaries must stay the same wherever you go with your dog.

1. Dogs do what you allow them to do and do not understand right from wrong unless they are taught through training.
2. All positive behaviors should be rewarded, and negative behaviors should be corrected.
3. Keep your training sessions short. Training is mentally exhausting for a dog. Some have short attention spans and get bored quickly.

It is important to pay attention to what you are rewarding. Rewarding is all about timing and looking for the exact behavior you expect. Here are a couple of tips to help you later.

1. Whether a command or your dog's name, do not continue to say the word over and over when you don't see the result you want.
2. Be sure that your dog is in the exact position you command before you reward.

Training is for Learning and Having Fun

Dogs learn by watching your body language and listening to your tone. When training, stay calm and pay attention to your hand and body positioning as well as your voice commands.

- Do not train if you are distracted or mad.
- Do not get frustrated if your dog does not understand what you are asking. Perhaps you need to change your approach.

Keep your training simple. You do not need to use extra words other than the commands. When you use too many words, your dog will get confused and frustrated.

- Always end your training on a positive note.
- Train your dog in different locations, either in your home or outside the home.
- Work your dog around distractions once they know the commands about 90% of the time.

It is important to make training fun. Your dog will learn quicker if you make training into a game.

Keep in mind that each dog, like people, learns at their own pace, and some need different motivation tools to keep training fun and interesting. Do not get discouraged if your dog does not learn as quickly as others.

Step 2
Creating Rules and Boundaries

Teaching your dog rules and boundaries takes consistency, but also leadership skills. There is such a thing as loving your dog too much, which means loving your dog so much that you don't correct negative behavior. The following are some of the outcomes for dogs without a leader.

1. Aggrcssion
2. Destructiveness
3. Anxiety
4. Fearfulness

Establish leadership for your dog to understand that you're the leader. Dogs are smart; they'll figure out what they can get away with, so never let your dog take advantage of you.

1. Training helps establish leadership.
2. Being strict with rules and boundaries is important anywhere you go with your dog.

Be sure everyone is on board with the same rules and boundaries.

Getting on the Same Page

Create a list of rules and boundaries and stick with them. This will help your dog learn exactly what you expect and what they expect from you in return, whether a reward or correction. Some questions to ask yourself about creating rules and boundaries are as follows.

- What rooms are my dog allowed in?
- Is my dog allowed on the furniture?
- What routines do I want for my dog throughout the day?
- Where will my dog sleep at night?
- Is my dog allowed to have table scraps?

It's also important to create rules and boundaries for yourself as well. Be sure that you and everyone else working with your dog are clear about safe and acceptable behaviors for your dog.

- Don't hit or yell at your dog. It will create fear and trust issues.
- Be sure that young children are interacting with the dog appropriately to avoid being afraid of children.
- Create an area where your dog can eat in peace. This avoids anxiety and food aggression.
- Don't leave your dog alone to eat or chew things that can harm them.

Tether your dog in the area where you are to avoid an opportunity for your dog to roam.

Step 3
Crate Training Fun

Crate training is an important part of the house-breaking process. It helps with potty training, rules and boundaries. Crates should never be used for punishment. Dogs typically love their crates, where they feel safe and secure.

1. Keep your dog in his crate overnight.
2. Keep your dog in the crate when you're not home.
3. Keep your dog in his crate when you're too busy to watch him.

In general, you may think, the bigger the crate, the better, because your dog will have more room. Wrong! With too much space, he will tend to potty on one side and sleep on the other. Give him just enough space to get up, turn around, and lie down again.

1. If your dog is a chewer, don't leave stuffed beds or toys in the crate to chew on.
2. Don't leave collars or chains on the dog when he's in the crate.
3. Leave a little water in a stainless steel bowl or a bottle at the side of the crate, along with an appropriate chewing toy.

The Crate is Your Dog's Safe Place

Crate training should be fun; your dog should feel comfortable going in and out on command any time. Crate games teach your dog that the crate is a good, safe place.

- Reward your dog for going into the crate.
- Reward your dog for sitting and waiting patiently to leave the crate.

Remember not to reward negative behavior, like barking or being overly excited in the crate, creating anxiety.

- When your dog goes into the crate, close it and walk away. Before he comes out, he should be calm and sitting quietly before you let him out.
- Cover the crate with something he can't pull through to chew on. This helps some dogs stay calmer.
- If your dog cries, don't let him out of the crate. He'll learn that if he cries, you will come to take him out and continue to cry whenever you put him in.
- Give frequent potty breaks; if they don't potty outside, put them back in the crate and try again soon.
- Be sure your dog gets sufficient exercise to help him stay calm in the crate.

Step 4
Proper Ways of Socializing Your Dog

When we think of socializing a dog, some believe this means to have their dog play with other dogs and kids. While some dogs may be fine with that, others can be traumatized.

1. Experiences must be positive, and good behavior must be rewarded.
2. Be aware of what you reward. Don't reward your dog when he's scared by petting or picking him up. Comforting him when he's scared rewards negative behavior. Try redirecting him and move on from the area.
3. Take your dog to new places after you have established good leadership.

There's a small window in a dog's development when they're most accepting of things around them. This is typically from three to 14 weeks old. That said, not all dogs are able to play with other dogs or children due to lack of exposure at early ages or for other reasons.

1. Walk your dog on a different route daily, with new scenery and people.
2. Introduction to other dogs must be slow.
3. Introduce your dog to kids who are respectful.

Leadership is Important in Socializing

Well-socialized dogs are typically more confident and less fearful when introduced to new experiences. The following are positive outcomes of having a well-socialized dog.

- Increases adaptability
- Less anxiety for you and your dog
- Enhances a bonding relationship
- Maintains positive mental health
- Prevents behavioral problems

You play a big role in socializing with your dog. The key is to be the confident leader your dog needs. Your dog will feel more secure. If you're nervous, your dog will feel uneasy, which creates fear.

- Watch your body position. Stand up straight and walk with purpose.
- Hold the leash with confidence and know that you're always in complete control.

It is important to understand the difference between socialization and just exposing your dog to different experiences. Exposure is when you introduce your dog to new things. More exposure at a very young age helps to build confidence and reduce fear. Socialization is the process of exposing your dog to new things and helping them learn how to interact with people, communicate with other dogs and feel comfortable in most situations.

Step 5
Deciding Commands

Choosing commands to teach your dog should not be a complicated process. It's important to keep it simple. Here you learn the basic commands you will use throughout the day to incorporate them into your daily routines.

1. Choose your commands carefully.
2. Everyone working with your dog must use the same commands to build and maintain a bond with your dog. This also ensures your dog's safety.

The words you choose help with teaching commands. You will use marker words and release words, which must be used consistently. A good example of a marker word is "good." A good example of a release word is "free."

1. The marker word marks the exact moment your dog is in the command position you asked of him.
2. The release word gives your dog permission to release himself from the command position he was in.
3. Do *not* use words for the marker or release words you say multiple times a day, such as, "Okay."

How to Use the Marker and Release Word

Whether you use English, German, or Spanish commands, it's important to clearly define the commands until you're certain that the correct behavior is associated with the command. The commands won't work if any of the following occurs.

- There's a lack of exact timing with the marker word or the release word.
- There's a lack of consistency using the marker word, the command, and the release word.

No matter what command you're teaching, it's all done in an easy sequence for your dog to understand. Below is an example of what teaching your dog a command might look like.

- Lure your dog into a sit by utilizing a treat when his back end is on the floor and both front paws are on the floor. Quickly mark the position by saying, "good," followed by the command, "sit," and followed up with a treat. Then you immediately use your release word, releasing the dog from a sit by saying, "free."
- If the dog gets up before you say the release word, lure him back into the command position without a reward and say the release word again.

Step 6
Luring Your Dog With Food Rewards

Luring your dog can be tricky at times and a bit frustrating. Dogs learn body language before they learn verbal language, making luring an easy way to teach commands.

1. To lure into position, have a highly-valued treat when your dog is learning.
2. Move your hand slowly to keep him calm and focused during luring.
3. Keep your hand low at head height so he doesn't feel the urge to jump up to get the treat.

Pay attention to your body language when you lure your dog into position with food. Your position is a crucial part of the lure. Keep your body in an upright position as much as possible.

1. Hold the treat in your hand, ensuring that your dog can't get it.
2. Bring your hand close to his nose and slowly lure him into the position you're looking for.
3. When your dog is in the exact position, mark it saying, "good," followed by the position command and reward with the treat. Then, use your release word, "free."

Luring Your Dog is Part of Learning

Luring is all part of learning. It's not bad to start with luring when you're teaching new commands, or if your dog is learning something new. Luring where there are many distractions is a good idea, especially in the beginning.

- Lures are used in the early stages of training.
- When a dog understands commands 90% of the time, start weaning the lure and treat.

Once a dog knows and truly understands a command, he won't need a treat every time. He should only be rewarded at that point when he makes good decisions on his own.

- A lure is not a reward. The reward comes when your dog has performed the command correctly.
- Do not reward your dog if he doesn't perform the command correctly.

Luring your dog is beneficial because it provides a clear visual for your dog to learn new behaviors and it is a positive motivator for them to learn faster and easier. You can use treats or a toy to direct them into the position you are teaching. Dogs are naturally motivated by food, and this is a positive training method to foster bonding between your dog and you, or training in new environments.

Step 7
Teach Your Dog to Sit

Teaching your dog to sit will come in handy in many different situations. This leads to an auto sit at crosswalks, when you stop to have a conversation with a friend, or any other situation when you may need your dog to sit even when you don't give the command. Here are the beginning steps to teaching the sit command.

1. With a treat in hand, place it in front of your dog's nose and slowly raise your hand up and over his head, luring him into a sit position.
2. Once your dog is in a sit, quickly mark it by saying, "good." Then say the verbal command, "sit," and reward with the treat, and use your release word, "free."
3. Be sure to use high-value rewards.

Here are a few other tips that go with the sit command.

1. Don't reward unless your dog's back end and paws are on the floor.
2. Don't say the word sit before you lure him into position.
3. Release immediately in the beginning.

Pay Attention When Rewarding

Sometimes, if you're not paying attention, you could be rewarding and teaching your dog negative behaviors. He should be rewarded for positive behaviors only. So, what is a proper sit?

- A proper sit is when your dog's back end and front paws are on the floor.
- Don't get frustrated; wait until your dog is in the correct position to give the command and the reward.

Whether you're teaching a puppy or an older dog, it's important to remember the following.

- Keep sit training short and fun, so your dog doesn't get bored.
- Incorporate the sit into your daily routines.

Another important key is when you are training your dog to sit, remember that the release word is just as important. If your dog gets up before you use the release word, lure your dog back into the sit position with no reward, and use the release word. This is to teach your dog to stay in that position until you tell him he is free to get out of that position. As time goes on, you will see that there will be more control from your dog's perspective to not be so rushed to get up.

Step 8
Teaching Your Dog to Down

There are many important reasons to teach your dog down, and in some cases, it could save your dog from injury or worse. The process of teaching your dog the down command is like the sit command. Here are the first steps to teach the command down.

1. With a treat in hand near the dog's nose, slowly lower your hand toward the floor, to the dog's chest, and then out in front of him in a fluid motion.
2. Once your dog is in a down, mark it with "Good," and say the command "down" as you reward him, then say, "free" to release.
3. Some dogs will get this right away, and for some, it can take days of trying.

Here are more tips for teaching the down position.

1. A true down means the elbows, belly, and backend are flat on the floor.
2. Watch that the back end doesn't come off the floor, because the back legs tend to spring up if they're not relaxed.
3. Release from this position quickly in the beginning.

Expectations for the Down Command

There are a couple ways you can train the down command. Some prefer their dog to be in a sphinxlike position. This could tempt the dog to spring up out of position. Some like their dog to be in a more relaxed position where the back legs are sprawled out. The following are some things to remember.

- Take your time, and don't get frustrated if your dog doesn't get this right away. Just watch what you reward by ensuring the correct position every time.
- The down command means to lie down. To get down off something, the command, "off" is used, meaning to get off an object or a person.

If your dog doesn't get it right away, you can try the following tricks of the trade to help.

- Use a prop such as a highchair rung to lure him under to force him into a down.
- Use a wood or vinyl floor to help your dog slide into position easily without thinking about it.

If your dog gets up from the down position before you release him, put him back in position without a reward and release him again. Don't allow him to get up from the position without the release word. It will be harder later on to teach him if you allow this.

Step 9
Teach Your Dog to Stay

At this stage of the game, given the work you've done so far, your dog is ready to learn to sit and down-stay. Even if your dog knows to sit and down 90% of the time, continue conditioning and reinforcing the commands separately. Stay is an important command, and timing is crucial. Below are the beginning steps to the sit-stay command.

1. Lure your dog into a sit position and reward. Hold the back of the collar so he can't lunge forward. Place a few treats on the floor in front of him.
2. Rapidly reward with treats, one at a time, saying, "Good, stay."
3. Use your release word to free him from the sit-stay.

Now try it for a down-stay. The steps are the same, except for the down command.

1. Lure your dog into a down position and reward. Hold the back of his collar so he can't lunge forward. Place a few treats on the floor in front of him.
2. Rapidly reward with treats, one at a time, saying, "Good, stay."
3. Use your release word to free him from the down-stay.

Take Your Time and Don't Rush

After using those steps for a week, stand in front of him and take one step back every day to create distance between you and your dog. These are the next steps for the sit and down-stay.

- Put him into the sit or down and reward. Tell him to stay.
- Take one step back, then one step forward. Reward and say, "Good, stay," and then "free."

Each day, take an extra step back. If your dog gets up when you back up, don't go as far the next time; he may not be ready for that distance. There are two more things to remember.

- Do not reward your dog if he gets up from the position.
- If your dog gets up and or inches toward you, bring him back to the exact spot you started at, and repeat again.

Be clear on whether you want your dog to sit or down-stay. If you ask him to sit and he lies down, bring him back to a sit. A frequent mistake is asking the dog to sit and then say down to get him in the down position. If you want him to go into a down, just lure him down. Eventually, you will be able to say down, but not rush the process. If your dog gets up from either position before release from the stay, lure him back into the position without a reward and use your release word.

Step 10
Teach Your Dog to Place

There are many reasons why place is important in everyday life. It may take a few weeks for your dog to understand, but remember that consistency is very important in teaching any command. Here are some steps to teach the place command using a leash.

1. Select a command. Use words such as place or bed.
2. Use a mat, a rug, or a bed to teach this command.
3. Lure your dog onto the mat, rug, or bed, and reward with a treat and say, "Good, place," and "free."

Do those first steps and shape the behavior for several days, then use the following steps.

1. Lure your dog onto the mat, rug, or bed and wait a little longer each time before rewarding and saying, "Good, place," and then "free."
2. You can start adding sit-stays and down-stays in place, then reward.
3. Add distance from place each day by stepping back then returning, rewarding, and saying, "Good, stay," and "free."

Place Has Many Benefits

Place is used to help establish rules and boundaries. It promotes relaxation and helps prevent negative behavior. It also creates a safe place for your dog in the following situations:

- When you're driving, at the veterinary office, or when they need to be safe due to an emergency.
- If you're busy and need your dog to be safe while you work.

This command can benefit a dog with behaviors such as being shy, nervous, demanding, and even separation anxiety. After your dog has learned this command, it's crucial to do the following.

- Add distractions a little at a time. Distractions include toys, food, children, or other animals.
- Practice training this command in different locations.

Step 11
Door Dashing

Have you ever opened the door carrying groceries, the dog runs out, knocks you over, the groceries go flying, and he's down the road before you even realize what happened? Yes, of course, you have, or maybe it was a similar situation. That's why the door dashing drill is great for training. It's an easy training routine your dog can learn quickly with consistent practice.

1. Wearing a leash, have your dog sit-stay at the door, and open it slowly.
2. Close the door and reward, saying, "Good, stay," then repeat twice.
3. The fourth time, repeat the step, but instead of closing the door, tell him, "free," and head out the door.

If your dog moves out of the sit-stay position, close the door, and start over as many times as necessary without rewards.

1. This training may not take long, but don't rush it.
2. Ensure that you have plenty of treats stashed near the door for this exercise.
3. This drill must be done even when you're running late.

Don't Set Your Dog Up for Failure

Never set your dog up for failure. This can happen when you're not thinking about all the important behaviors you expect from your dog, be it training or everyday routines. Other helpful training tips for this drill include the following.

- Have your dog sit at the side of the door and when it opens, he doesn't move at all.
- Before you allow them to "free" out the door, make a habit of looking outside to ensure it's safe for them to go out.

Door dashing training is good in various situations, whether he's in the car, the crate, or any other door he has to go through to exit or enter. This is especially beneficial for the following.

- When people come to visit using the front door, be aware that dogs can knock people over and cause unintended injuries.
- Be sure to watch your dog at the door if you live near a road.
- Also, be aware that if you live near an area with wild animals, they may come close to the house.

Step 12
The Leave-It Command

This command is different than the drop it command. The purpose of this command is for your dog to leave an item, person, or place (i.e., a room) alone. Here are the first steps to teach this drill as follows.

1. On leash, have your leave-it treats in one hand and the reward in another.
2. With a tightly-closed fist low to the dog's nose, offer the leave-it treats, while hiding the reward behind your back in the opposite hand.
3. As soon as your dog looks away for any reason or a distraction of any kind, reward with the reward hand only and say, "Good, leave it."

Repeat by offering the closed-fist leave-it treats again. Look for these signs from your dog even in the first session.

1. Your dog will start looking for the reward.
2. The dog may completely ignore the leave-it-treat hand.
3. The dog may start to back away from the leave-it-treat hand.

Leave It Alone

Your dog may act like he knows this command after a short period of time, but in a real situation, it might be a different story. Use this drill in real-life routines and situations. Remember the following points during training.

- Even if your dog looks away every time, continue the drill.
- Even if your dog backs away and ignores your leave-it-treat hand completely, continue working the drill.

This command can save your dog's life by staying away from unfriendly dogs or people. It can also be used to get them to ignore something that could be harmful to them, or to keep your dog from hurting someone.

Examples can include the following:

- Trash, debris, or hazardous items like medicine, candy, or chicken bones.
- Children running around, possibly with food.

A command can also be taught while you're playing fetch. After you throw the ball and he brings it back, you can ask him to drop it. He will drop the ball out of his mouth. Now you want to tell him to leave it so he doesn't go to grab it as you reach for it. This is especially important when a child wants to play fetch with their dog.

Step 13
The Drop-It Command

Have you ever dropped something on the floor and before you could pick it up, your dog was right there to seize it? Was it something hot, spicy, or poisonous? Teaching your dog to drop it is important for his safety. Here are steps to teach your dog to drop it.

1. Pick a toy your dog likes to play with. You will also need a high-value treat.
2. While on a leash, allow your dog to play with the toy for a minute.
3. Put the treat near the dog's nose and as soon as he drops it, say, "Good, drop-it," and reward. Continue repeating this drill.

Here are some tips to keep in mind.

1. If your dog doesn't drop the toy, don't take it out of his mouth. Instead, stay calm and try to distract him with the reward.
2. Avoid yelling or punishment. You want this to be a positive experience while he's learning this command.
3. It takes patience, repetition, and consistency to teach your dog to drop it.

Drop-It Isn't Leave-It

There's a big difference between the drop-it command and the leave-it command. Use them in conjunction with each other. After he drops it, you want him to leave it.

- The drop-it command is intended to have him drop what's in his mouth.
- Use the leave-it command when you want him to leave it after he drops it, or before he takes it.

Teaching drop-it should be fun for both you and your dog. You can play games such as tug or fetch while you're teaching this command and thereafter. You will need treats in the beginning, but the toy will eventually be the reward.

- Throw a ball, have your dog fetch it, and bring it back. Say, "Drop-it," and reward.
- Play tug with your dog for a minute or two, then have him "drop-it," and reward.

If you have a dog with guarding issues, teaching the "drop it" command is crucial. It will provide a safe and controlled way to remove an item they are guarding, preventing potential aggression or biting. It allows you to manage their behavior by exchanging the guarded item with a positive reward.

Step 14
The Leash Walking Drill

Who doesn't like walking their dog on a beautiful day, or taking their dog to events? Your dog will need to walk properly on a leash to enjoy the outing. And surprise—your dog needs to learn from his training! There are many tools you can use for this. Every dog is different and may need different tools to learn. Here are a few popular tools from my training program.

1. A flat collar, a Martingale collar, or a harness
2. A prong collar, also known as a pinch collar
3. An E-collar

All tools are safe if used properly and you've been professionally trained to use them. These are the first steps to teach a dog to leash walk. Start indoors with minimal distractions.

1. Get a handful of high-value rewards.
2. Walk your dog on the same side as the hand with treats, and the leash in your opposite hand to avoid him walking in front of you.
3. With treats at his nose, walk forward to lure him. Reward often as you walk.

Leash Walking is Good for Bonding

Here are a couple of tips to teach your dog to walk properly on a leash.

- Keep your hand low to your dog's nose to avoid jumping for the treat.
- If your dog goes ahead of you, lure him back by walking back a couple of steps, then lure him again to your side and back into position; then start walking again.

Once your dog gets the hang of it, you can stand upright and reward periodically. If he looks at you consistently, he's focused on you. Go outside and start working. It may seem like starting over, but that's due to distractions. Start with small distractions and work your way up to large ones. Parks, trails, and stores are all good places to train. While you're training in public, remember the following training tips.

- Don't allow anyone to pet or play with your dog during training. Simply explain that he's in training.
- People may judge you for using certain training tools. Just remember the tool you use works for your dog, and it's safe and effective. Don't engage with people who lecture you about tool safety.

Even if you do not plan to bring your dog on walks, it is still important to teach leash walking. He will need it to go to the vet or other places at some point.

Step 15
The Importance of Exercise

Exercise is good for dogs for many different reasons. It improves their physical and mental health and prevents injuries as well.

1. Most dogs need at least 30 to 60 minutes each day, and sometimes more.
2. Just running around in the backyard to sniff and potty isn't proper exercise. They need to play fetch and run hard, or take a brisk walk around the block or on a trail to consider it as adequate exercise.
3. Certain dog breeds need more exercise than others. Consider this before you get a dog. If you have one already, research the breed and find out what they need to be happy and healthy.

If you start to see behavioral issues, it could mean your dog isn't getting enough exercise, and you should work it into your schedule before the behaviors worsen. Pay attention to the following signs.

1. Your dog is destructive and chews everything.
2. Your dog is anxious and often whines.
3. Your dog shows signs of aggression.

Sniffing is Exercise for the Brain

There are benefits to walking your dog, aside from its physical and mental aspects. Walking your dog can also help with the following two points.

- Being active and having fun with your dog will strengthen your bond.
- This can be a great way to socialize your dog in public.

Believe it or not, when your dog sniffs, his brain is being exercised. Sniffing provides mental stimulation by engaging his highly developed sense of smell, allowing him to gather and interpret information about his environment, which requires concentration and cognitive effort.

- Sniffing can be calming and helps reduce canine anxiety.
- There are scent-work classes for dogs that encourage sniffing, so you both enjoy having fun in class together.

Along with sniffing classes, there are many other sports you can look into for your dog, or there may be a local pool/lake for him to swim. Some of these sports may include dock diving, disc, agility, fly ball, lure coursing, rally, barn hunt, or herding. Some breeds will be better than others at these sports, but it's a good way to get your dog exercise, build his confidence, and you will have a fun-filled day with your dog.

You've finished. Before you go...

Post/Share that you finished this book.

Please star rate this book.

Reviews are solid gold to writers. Please take a few minutes to give us some itty bitty feedback.

ABOUT THE AUTHOR

At a very young age, Melissa showed interest in animals and working with them; dogs and horses in particular. In 10th grade, she made a business plan in English class for a doggy daycare spa and cafe she would one day own. Many years later, her dreams came true.

She opened her doggy day camp and training business after completing a dog training certification program. Working with many trainers, mentors, and volunteering at shelters, Melissa found that this was her passion and wanted to pursue her dream.

Since starting her dog training career, Melissa has helped hundreds of dogs in rescue, families, and even her employees to thrive. She understands how important dogs are to people and that sometimes families struggle to get the training help they need for their dog.

This book is intended to help families who struggle with training needs for their dog, with step-by-step guidance to train your dog even with a strict budget and schedule.

Melissa's dream is to continue helping dogs and their families to live happy and healthy lives together in peace and harmony.

Together, a difference can be made. Training is for life.

If you enjoyed this Itty Bitty™ book, you might also like…

- **Your Amazing Itty Bitty™ Keep Your Children Safe Book -** Lynda J. Bergh Herring

- **Your Amazing Itty Bitty™ Be the Boss Now Book -** Gregory Allan Datu Cendana

- **Your Amazing Itty Bitty™ Legendary Leadership Academy Handbook** - Ed Nicholls, Jr.

Or any of the many Amazing Itty Bitty™ books available online at
www.ittybittypublishing.com

www.ingramcontent.com/pod-product-compliance
Lightning Source LLC
Chambersburg PA
CBHW060949050426
42337CB00052B/3286